A GUIDE TO THE MARIJUANA RUSH

Ray Robinson

A GUIDE TO THE MARIJUANA RUSH

©2017

Ray Robinson
www.riseofhealthconsciousness.com
Email: riseofhealthconsciousness@yahoo.com

Table of Contents

Disclaimer

Investing involves substantial risk. All information provided herein is for informational purposes only, not intended for trading purposes or advice and does not constitute recommendations or endorsements of any issuer, security or action.

While some of the information herein is from sources believed to be reliable, the author does not warrant their completeness and accuracy and should not be relied upon as such when making investment decisions.

In addition, the author doesn't make any guarantee as to any results that are obtained from its content.

The author shall not be responsible for updating or correcting any information or opinion contained herein. No reader should make any investment decision without first consulting his or her own personal financial advisor and conducting his or her own research and due diligence.

Neither the author nor any of his affiliates is liable for any informational errors or for any actions taken in reliance on information contained herein.

Dedication

This book is dedicated to all of my family, friends and supporters. I hope that you find this book informative and that it helps you and your family achieve your financial goals.

1

Introduction

Peace my name is Ray Robinson I am a former financial advisor. I worked on Wall Street as financial advisor for about two years. In those two years I learned an enormous amount of information regarding the stock market and how it functions.

In this book you will learn the basics of the stock market. I will also guide you on how to buy your first share of stock.

Due to the nature of the current climate in the stock market many other investors and analysts are targeting the marijuana sector. The marijuana sector is projected to be worth 40 billion by the year 2020! At the moment, marijuana is still considered illegal at the federal level but about 9 states have fully legalized it for recreational use; whereas, about half of the country has legalized it for its medical use.

With that being said there seems to be great potential for the average person to make alot of money by investing in marijuana companies. Many of them are trading for just pennies. Many traders are calling it the marijuana rush and it's supposed to be bigger than the Smartphone industry of the early 2000's. While I do not agree with smoking marijuana I definitely acknowledge the many health benefits of it, in forms such as edibles, teas etc.

I agree with people's right to chose though and many states have also agreed and legalized it. I think within the next five years America will legalize marijuana in all states. Canada and many other western countries are heading in that direction. This is not a get rich scheme; this is an opportunity to change your life. Many of us have IRA's 401k's etc and no investment knowledge.

This booklet will give you basic information that you can use to gain understanding of how the markets work; and maybe, help you make some of your own investment decisions.

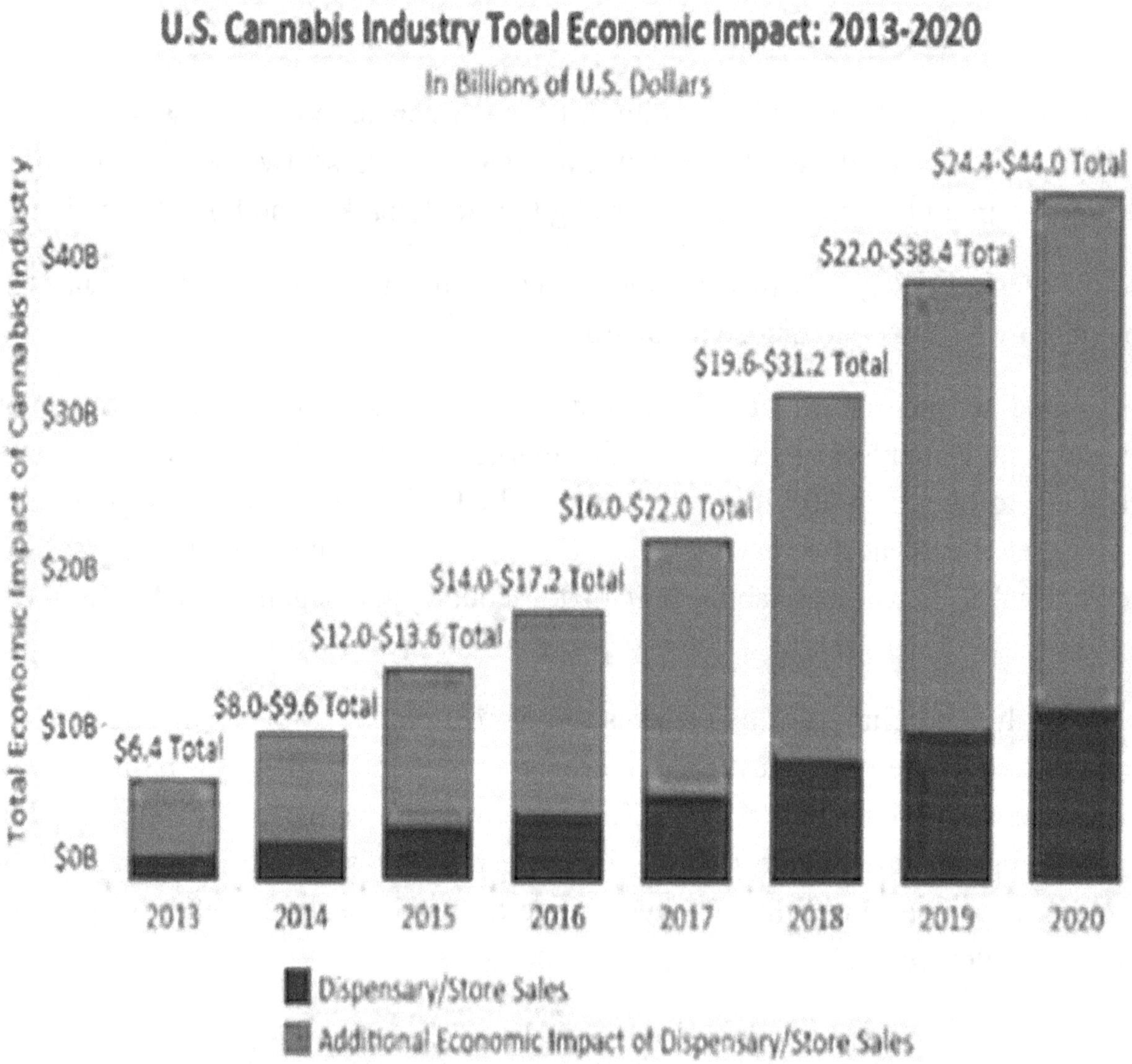

U.S. Cannabis Industry Total Economic Impact: 2013-2020
In Billions of U.S. Dollars

Total Economic Impact of Cannabis Industry

- $6.4 Total (2013)
- $8.0-$9.6 Total (2014)
- $12.0-$13.6 Total (2015)
- $14.0-$17.2 Total (2016)
- $16.0-$22.0 Total (2017)
- $19.6-$31.2 Total (2018)
- $22.0-$38.4 Total (2019)
- $24.4-$44.0 Total (2020)

■ Dispensary/Store Sales
■ Additional Economic Impact of Dispensary/Store Sales

My time as a stock broker

After being laid off from my job at the museum, I was determined to get into the Stock market industry anyway that I could. Being that I had no prior experience in finance or any college degrees it was hard to even get an interview for anything related to the stock market. What helped me out was doing a temporary customer service job for a brokerage firm.

After doing that job I was a little more marketable to enter the industry but being that I had no college degree there was only one position that I could get. That position was a stock broker, a stock broker is nothing but a salesperson, and he doesn't have to know anything about the stock market the only thing he needs to know is how to sell.

I worked in what would be considered a small boiler room. My managers were great sales people and they would say anything in order to get a guy to by a stock. From what I expected and what the reality was of being a broker was very different. Being a broker in this modern day where most people have caller ID's and have been burned by stock brokers over the phone or other people selling things makes the job difficult. The job was only calling from 8-4pm, I made about 2-300 calls a day. I used this time to learn about the market, my managers were also investors.

I listened to their conversations and began studying on my own and applying what I learned. I opened up a few accounts that went to my managers before leaving and finding a better sales job. But what I learned from the hardest sales job in the world will stay with me for life. Imagine calling up a complete stranger asking them to send you $10-20,000 after speaking to them for 60 seconds? They told me in the old era people were excited to get a cold call and invest. My experience was being hung up and cursed out.

There was also a guy who didn't know what he was getting into by becoming a stock broker; he quit 2 months after becoming licensed. I stayed with the firm for about a year and a half. Being that my managers made about $30k each a month they weren't that interested in pushing any new people up to that level. So I would call lead sheets with names of people who died in the 1990's. Even though it didn't work out I still thank them for the opportunity.

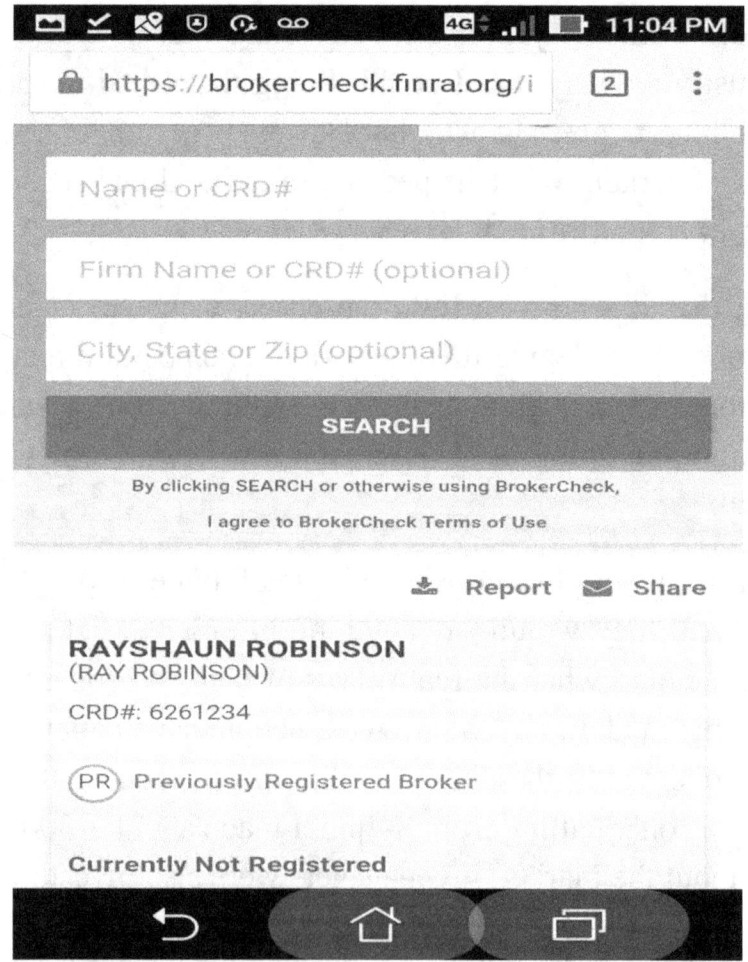

3

What is the stock market and how does it work?

The stock market is exactly as it sounds; it's a market that lets average people participate in the achievements or failures of companies. Many people falsely believe that companies are owned by executives and CEO's but actually all companies that trade on a stock exchange are owned by investors.

These investors then elect who they want to run and manage the company that they own. Every trading day billions of dollars are made and lost, in 2013 it was estimated that average trading daily value was $169 billion. Normal trading hours are from 9.30-4pm and the market is broken down into what are called exchanges.

The main slogan of the stock market is "buy low and sell high." This is much harder than most would think, because while you may have your money in a particular company and looking for it to go up there are people on the other side of your trade with their money hoping it goes down. The winner will be determined by if there are more buyers than sellers.

The stock market is run on the basic economic principle of whatever alot of people want will cause it to rise in value, and the things people are staying away from or selling will cause it to decrease in value. The stock market is a battle between the bulls and bears (buyers and sellers); the bulls are buying for an increase in share value while the bears are shorting (selling) to bring down the value.

The things that make stocks move are earnings releases, news releases and investor's emotions. Investor's emotions are what cause a stock to be overbought or oversold. A stock that is really worth $50 a share based on valuation can be trading at $80 just by investors pushing it up based on how they feel about it.

The market always corrects itself and when it corrects itself you are either rewarded or punished by what side of the trade that you are on. The stock market is not a get rich scheme, I've heard from people who lost $300,000 before becoming a profitable trader or investor.

Marijuana health benefits, history of use and how it became illegal

Marijuana has been used for thousands of years throughout the world by various cultures. Rameses the second who died in 1213 B.C was mummified with cannabis honey. Prescriptions for cannabis in Ancient Egypt included treatment for glaucoma, inflammation, cooling the uterus, administering enemas and much more.

Cannabis is another word for marijuana in fact, the word "marijuana" is what prohibition supporters called cannabis as they sought to demonize its use and criminalize its consumers. From 1850-1937 marijuana was used to treat over 100 illnesses in the U.S. But in the 1930's, Racist propaganda began to spread about men of color.

Harry Anslinger, the first commissioner of the Federal Bureau of Narcotics (an early predecessor of the DEA), was one of the driving forces behind pot prohibition. He pushed it for explicitly racist reasons, saying, "Reefer makes darkies think they're as good as white men," and: "There are 100,000 total marijuana smokers in the U.S., and most are Negroes, Hispanics, Filipinos and entertainers. Their Satanic music, jazz and swing result from marijuana use.

This marijuana causes white women to seek sexual relations with Negroes, entertainers and any others." In 1937 the "Marijuana Tax Act" essentially outlawed the possession or sale of marijuana. But in 1970 the supreme held the 1937 marijuana tax act to be unconstitutional. However in 1972 marijuana was placed on the list of controlled substances. Specifically it was listed with heroin, LSD, ecstasy and others, which are all considered by the federal government to have no medicinal properties and fall under what's called schedule one drugs.

The first state to legalize medical marijuana was California in 1996. Medical marijuana is used in many states today to treat many illnesses such as HIV, cancer, asthma, glaucoma, inflammation and much more. Also in 2012 Colorado and Washington became the first states to fully legalize marijuana for adults 21 and over. This has opened the flood gates to a huge industry, Colorado made so much money from marijuana in 2015 that it gave some of it back to tax payers.

Then there's hemp which is in the same family of marijuana, instead of being smoked and eaten in brownies etc, hemp can be used as paper, fuel, bricks and can even be eaten. Hemp seeds are very high in protein and omega fatty acids. The main difference between hemp and marijuana is that hemp doesn't contain THC which is the psychoactive ingredient in marijuana that gets you intoxicated.

The difference between investors and traders

Investors and traders take the opposite approach in the stock market. Investors in most cases actually believe in the companies that they invest in and don't mind holding onto their positions for months and even years. While traders care nothing about companies they are only concerned with making a few points which can take a few second or minutes. Even if these points are made off of rumors and speculation that they can quickly capitalize on. Investors will look more at a company's balance sheet, quarterly and annual earnings where as traders rely mostly on charts to see if an opportunity to buy or short presents itself.

I think the best way to approach the market is to be a mix of both. Knowing which stocks to buy or short based on what's going on fundamentally and when to do it based on charts and rumors. Believe it or not rumors are very powerful in the stock market. I've seen stocks increase or decrease drastically in one day based solely on rumors. Only to correct the price after the rumor has been verified to be false. An example of this can be a rumor that Apples' next I-Phone will be able to scan people's brains and read their thoughts I know it sounds farfetched but you get the point. Something like that can cause apple stock to increase just as a negative rumor can cause it decrease.

Traders sometimes also use a company's earnings release as an opportunity to buy or short. A company's earnings release can be a very volatile time for a stock it can increase or decrease drastically in a short period of time based on if the numbers came in as analyst expected, exceeded or under than what was expected. But it's not so clear cut; a company can report bad quarterly earnings but still increase based on a forward guidance or something that was said on a conference call which can leave investors feeling optimistic about the company's future. The opposite of this is also true as good earnings don't automatically mean an increase in a stock performance. Sometimes a stock may not move at all or very little during an earnings release.

Another thing that mostly traders look for is a company's short interest ratio. Anything over 40% is an indicator that traders think that the company will be going down in value soon. One of the favorite sectors for traders to get involved in is Bio Technology. Bio Tech stocks are probably the most volatile out of all stocks in the market, I have seen some Bio Tech stocks go from $2 to 100 and back to $5 all in a few days. They are for the most daredevil speculators, a company might say they have a drug that can help manage or even cure cancer this can cause a massive influx of investors but when reality sets in and their claim is not true it could cause the stock to crash and the company may even go out of business.

6

How to go about buying stocks

In this modern era majority of business is done online, years ago to buy a stock you had to call a broker directly or wait for them to call you and recommend a stock. Today everything is online you can find out about a company A-Z. There are lots of online stocks trading platforms such as Sharebuilder, TD Ameritrade, Merrill Edge, Fidelity, etc. You will go to one of those sites and sign up.

You have to fill out your tax information, fund your account; then you are good to go. On these platforms you will have tools that help you select stocks based on their price, perceived risk, overall rating etc. This is how it works; if a stock is 10 cents you can buy about 9 shares for a dollar plus your commission fee which you will pay to the online broker that you bought the stock through. Your hope is that it when you buy it at 10 it goes up to 11 and beyond. You can also bet against stocks which they call "shorting".

When you short a stock you are hoping that the value decreases. You can sell the stocks you bought at any time after buying them. But there are some tax penalties that you may incur if you sell it within a year of purchase; your broker will explain all of this in detail. When you are at the section of your brokers' platform where you can buy stocks you will see the option of which stock you want, whether you want to buy or short, the current price and how many shares you will want. Many of them offer demo accounts so you can experiment before you use real cash.

The price of stocks fluctuates throughout the day. You can always check your personal account or you can check just do a simple Google search of your stock to see how it's doing throughout the day. Some things that can cause a stock's value to increase or decrease are rumors; companies expected growth or decline, and much more. It's always good to do a simple Google search of your company to see if they have any new news updates about them that may affect the current price of the stock.

7

What are stock charts and how to read them?

Stocks charts are a very important tool for investing in the stock market while this short book will focus majority on the marijuana sector. Those who can read charts can be successful in any sector or financial market.

There are many financial markets such as forex, options and bonds. Charts can be used for an indication for when there is a good place to buy a stock or when it's good to sell it. The two basic patterns in reading charts are m's and w's.

If a chart is forming an M it might be a good time to sell and if it's a W might be a good time to buy. Those are the basic chart patterns there are courses that deal with the intricate parts of chart reading many can be found online.

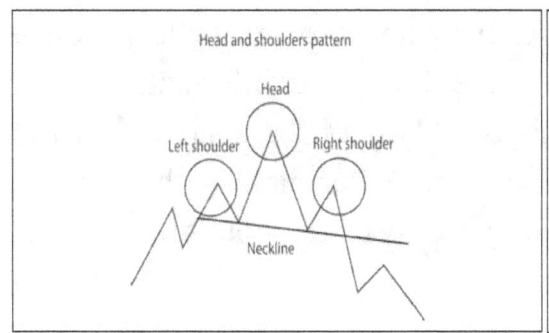

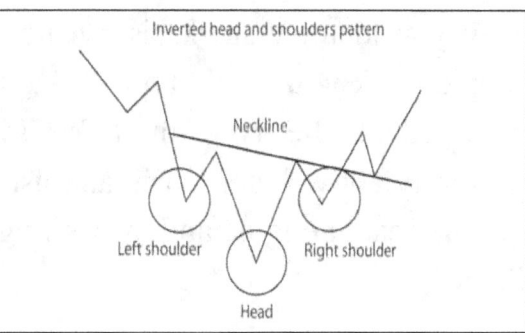

List of Marijuana stocks to watch

The way you find information about stocks is online. You can find out what traders are speaking about on twitter, for instance. You can also do a simple Google search of for example "top marijuana stocks." You need also to find likeminded people who also share the interest of stock trading and you all can pass around ideas.

I have compiled a list of companies that I think will turn out good. I have targeted "penny stocks." Penny stocks are stocks that trade below $5 a share. Right now a good majority of marijuana stocks trade in what is called the OTC market. OTC stands for over the counter, they have not made it to the bigger exchanges yet such as Nasdaq or the Dow. Penny stocks are considered extremely risky; hence, do your research before buying these or ANY stock.

The way you identify stocks is by their ticker symbol, for example if you're looking for apple stock you would type in Aapl to either buy or get information about it; below I will provide the list of the ticker symbols. Many of these stocks exist in states that currently allow legal marijuana use. Put the ticker symbol with the word stock in an online search engine and everything you need to know about the company will be available.

Even though all of these companies businesses revolve around marijuana, there are a bunch of different things that these companies are doing to profit in this sector. For example there are companies that are growing it, some are doing construction on the growth facilities, some are inspecting the quality, and some are hemp companies.

The different types of companies are vast, it's on you to know exactly what a company does and if you think they will be successful based on what you read about them and what their balance sheet and financials say about them.

The List
Ticker symbols

ERBB

MCIG

SGBY

MCOA

MJNA

CBIS

ETST

VAPE

TBP

STWC

AGTK

GBLX

BLO

GWPH

CNBX

MLFF

CVSI

TRTC

AXIM

ARNA

PHOT

MLCG

PURA

You are definitely encouraged to research and find more, but if you study that list in my opinion you will definitely find some big winners.

Frequently asked questions

How much money will I make?

It is not guaranteed that you will make anything when buying stocks. It is an investment you only make money if the stock's value increases. There is also a chance that you will lose everything that you invested.

How long should I hold my stock?

There is no limit as to how long you can hold a stock, day traders may hold for seconds or minutes. But those who are serious investors intend to hold a stock long term or until they feel the stock has reached its peak. When you sell your stock you can sell a portion of it and hold the rest or you can sell all of your shares.

How many shares should I buy?

You should buy the amount you can afford; also the great thing about many of the marijuana stocks is that they are trading for pennies. This gives the average person the ability to purchase a large amount of shares for a low cost.

Conclusion

You are now equipped with the tools of understanding the basics of the stock market. Make sure to download apps on your phone like Net Dania or other apps that track the stock market.

Use yahoo finance and Google to find out information regarding particular company's financials, news and current earnings. This strategy was designed for marijuana penny stocks but this foundation can be used in any sector.

The question of when should you sell is up to you, nobody can decide that for you. We all have different goals some people hold stocks for days, weeks, and months of even years. This is your beginning trading. May you make alot of money!

Thanks for your purchase of the book, remember **www.riseofhealthconsciousness.com is here for your support. Send all questions and concerns to riseofhealthconsciousness@yahoo.com**